Some Short Poems of Life, Vol.1

Feather, To Ink, To Paper

By; Leon Edwards

Table of Context

List of Short Poems

Aquarius

Aquarius

January 20 - February 18

Symbol: The Water Bearer

Ruling Planet: Uranus, Ruling House: Eleventh of networking

Key Traits: Humanitarian, eccentric, individualistic, cool

The End is the Start of a New Adventure

A New Beginning

(2020)

(Life,s Cycle)

Pisces

Pisces
February 19 - March 20

Symbol: The Fish

Ruling Planets: Neptune

Ruling House: Twelfth House of Spirituality

Key Traits: Empathic, artistic, psychic, dreamy

(Counting the Rings of Time)

I Dedicate This Book of Poems
To My
Family and Friends for Their Love and Support

The Dream

Out of nowhere you came, since that day I knew it
Wouldn't be the same.
Searching the sky so blue I didn't know it would be you.
Your eyes where so clear and full of fight I knew this time it
Was just right.
Once I realize what was done the dream was over and so was
the fun.

The Child

Remembering myself as a child those times to me now were
really wild.
Riding bikes and climbing trees were the only important thing
to me.
Now I'm Grown and understand what it takes to be a man,
sooner than later you will find that the child you knew was
one of a kind.
So whatever you plan to do, just know that, that child is
still in you.

Aries

Aries
March 21 - April 19

Symbol: The Ram

Ruling Planet: Mars

Ruling House: First House of Self

Key Traits: Competitive, energetic, impulsive, fearless

The Wish

At the edge of a cliff one day, I wish I had wings to fly away.
High and Deep in the clouds I would go, Bouncing back and
forth with no thoughts of where I should go.
As the wind bends my wings, I felt a feeling and started to
sing.
The sound is so peaceful I started to think, to dive at the
lake to have a drink.
Resting on a limb of a tree, I often wish that it was me.

The Thought

Once a long time ago I had a thought it was time to go.
Somewhere New, Somewhere Fresh, I just know I needed
the rest.
Now and then you will see that it's still a part of me.
Now it's over, thinking too much will burn you out.

The Feeling

If you could see a Feeling what would you see?
If you look real hard you can see me.
Sometimes it's hard to understand all the rules of the land.
Filled with flower here they stand, causing a special
feeling in the land.

JM 2·9·10

Love

When the sky is clear and the air is clean, the smell of a new life
Is in the wings, waiting to spring.
Like the ocean of things to be, I welcome this change most willingly.
You are the reason in my life, so let's keep trying, you know I'm right.
So the only thing we need to do is wait for love to see us through.

Free

My soul is flying around the rim of time somehow destiny made you
mind. I haven't felt this way before, I knew one day
it would be much more. So all I need to make it right, is one
hundred days to spend the night. If you haven't figured out
by this time, I am your and you are mind.

Taurus

Taurus
April 20 - May 20

Symbol: The Bull-Ruling House:2nd,house of Income
Ruling Planet: Venus

Key Traits: Resolute, grounded, tenacious, sensual

I Wonder

As the thunder slaps the sky it makes me wonder why. All the things
that we go through and the many things still left to do.
Sitting at the window edge, hours go by, it's time for bed. But before I
do I look to the sky and still can't help but wonder why.

The Raising

Have you ever thought of the parents you had, a loving Mother and a
strong Dad. All of this seems so long ago, but now I know it's really
not so. Picking apart the pass I know, what their plan was to make me
grow. Other ways might have been right, but I was the kind to put up a
fight. Now, whatever I do in my life I always know that they were right.

Choices

The choices we make in life, Sometime wrong, Sometimes right.
Battling the beast inside, will take you on a long wild ride. Coming so
close to the end of the road, you come to find, you still don't know.
Life is a Beautiful thing it true, but the choices you make will pull you
through.

I See,

Seeking life the way I do, outside reality sometimes will do. Oftentimes I have to laugh, flashing back to the past. Take a minute and find yourself, never be afraid to ask for help. Having that person who will share, never judge and is always there.

Gemini

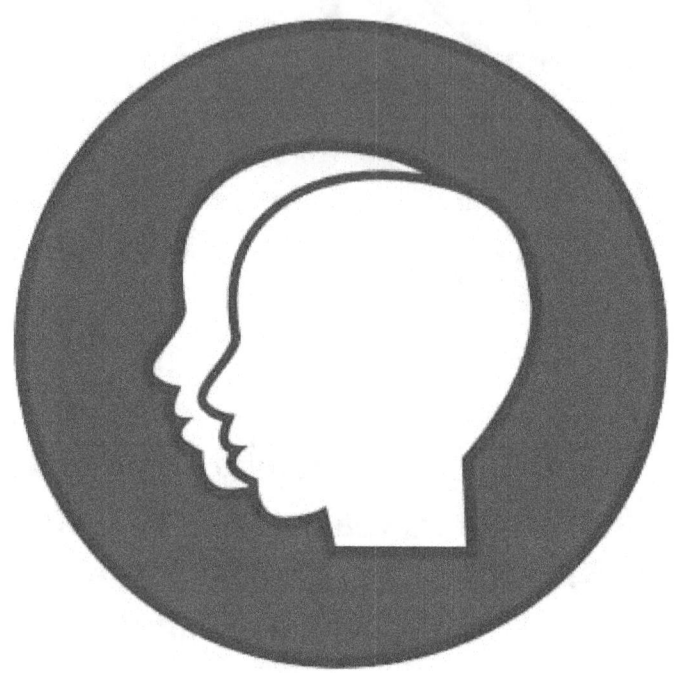

Gemini
May 21 - June 20

Symbol: The Twins

Ruling Planet: Mercury

Ruling House: Third House of Communication

Key Traits: Witty, curious, charming, flighty

A Rest,

How many times can we go through the uphill fight to achieve the right to control your life. Forgetting the rest, Taking the pressure off your mind and chest will give your life a much needed rest.

The Chance

If you had the chance to change your life, what would it take to make it right. Changing might be a mistake, is that the chance you want to take. Or would you give up the chance to change and be satisfied to remain the same. This question I give to you, if you had the chance what would you do.

Faith

Counting down the hours in a day, hoping the fear will stay away. Sometimes not knowing how it will end, ready for the next day to begin. Days, weeks and months go by sitting with the thoughts of things gone by. The power you seek is within yourself, having the faith, the courage and belief in yourself. If you dont think this is true, you need more faith in what you do.

Cancer

Cancer
June 21 - July 22

Symbol: The Crab

Ruling Planet: Moon

Ruling House: Fourth House of Home Life

Key Traits: Compassionate, giving, sentimental, nurturing

Leaving

Is leaving so hard to do, when the person you're with won't help you through, all the problems that you face, confidence down, feeling out of place. You look for another to fill that space. Thinking that you're having fun giving yourself to everyone. But the real thing you need to do is find peace and love that's true to you.

The Tree

When the wind blows the leaf of a tree, it's like an alarm clock to reality. Branches bend flower too, and the grass is like a wavy sea. Standing in the storm my body easily conforms. When the wind hits my brow it touches my heart and makes me smile. All this, standing next to a tree, try it one day and you will see.

Leo

Leo
July 23 - August 22

Symbol: The Lion

Ruling Planet: Sun

Ruling House: Fifth House of Romance and Self-Expression

Key Traits: Charismatic, generous, optimistic, dramatic

Offspring

Is there anything more beautiful to see, then a lovely baby to bounce on your knee, rather boy or girl born to this world, a fantastic scene for anyone to see. Taking care can be a chore, but the joy is worth, oh much more, seeing them grow and play, is a beautiful end to a long hard day.

A Story

Here's a story about a man, the richest, most handsomest man in the land. With all the women, at his beck and call, this guy knew he had it all. But it was one woman in the land that made his knees buckle where he stands. She was as lovely as a sunny day without him knowing she went away. The moral of this story I must say, speak up when that special person comes your way. It is possible that they might stay.

Virgo

Virgo
August 23 - September 22

Symbol: The Virgin or Maiden

Ruling Planet: Mercury

Ruling House: Sixth House of Wellness and Daily Routine

Key Traits: Health-conscious, analytical, service-oriented, detail-focused

Mother

Mother was a Delight to see, her smile, her walk is burned in my memory. Thinking of the things she went through, but the things she did was because of you. A special lady indeed, always pushing us to succeed. Never being able to pay the price to the beautiful woman that gave me life.

Sometimes

Coming across people in my life, some are nice and some will fight. With no thoughts of what they do, certain things they blame on you. All the while with a smile, but not really true to you. All I'm saying at the end, is sometimes it's hard to find a friend.

Libra

Libra
September 23 - October 22

Symbol: The Scales

Ruling Planet: Venus

Ruling House: Seventh House of Partnership

Key Traits: Romantic, artistic, indecisive, diplomatic

Partners

Looking for a partner in life, finding the lady to be your wife. Dating this one, that one, just won't do. Still looking for the one that's made for you. Coming to the conclusion that you are right, it's really hard to find a wife. Remembering dating the way you do every woman is not a lady, it's true. So don't give up that search in life to find the lady that will be your wife.

Reason

Up, Up, Up, we go, trying to find the reason to know. Searching for this reason for flight, keeps many scientists up at night. In their search they will see, some things are not meant to be. Rockets Boom and Planes explode, the fight goes on for that pot of gold. Round and round we go you see, life is still a mystery.

One Night

What do you say about the moon at night, the size, the color, the spiritual light. Sometimes people stop and stare, can't help but wonder who's out there. Some say yes, some say no, but honestly we just don't know. So admirer the moon from where you are, and don't forget to wish on a star.

The Path

Tow the line pull real hard, don't forget who you are. As we take the trail of life, trying real hard to make it right. Staying on the trail can be ruff, jumping hurdle and all that stuff. Most agree when I say, staying on the path is hard today. Believe in yourself, this is true, and happiness and success will come to you.

Scorpio

Scorpio
October 23 - November 21

Symbol: The Scorpion

Ruling Planets: Pluto and Mars

Ruling House: Eighth House of Emotional Bonds and Sexual Intimacy

Key Traits: Mysterious, magnetic, power-seeking, spiritual

Take the Time

The wonders of life are easy to see, take the time to touch a tree. Smell a rose and you will see how close to mother earth you will be. Some take it for granite there it be, the wonders of smelling a rose and touching a tree.

Winter Snow

Back and forth I'm going today, shoveling snow to make away. Down the sidewalk to the driveway, I look up for a minute and then I say Merry Christmas to a neighbor passing my way. Going back in the house cold as can be, happy that day is near, you see. The kids are happy in their beds, none of them can sleep, all looking for that slead. The day is here I'm sure you know, Enjoy your Christmas and the snow.

Sagittarius

Sagittarius
November 22 - December 21

Symbol: The Archer

Ruling Planet: Jupiter

Ruling House: Ninth House of Adventure and Higher Learning

Key Traits: Philosophical, free-spirited, unfiltered, wanderlusting

Ocean Breeze

Standing by the ocean catching the breeze, looking around at the beautiful sites to see. With the sand under your feet, and where you lay you, gather yourself for a relaxing day. As you do you will find that the site of the ocean is one of a kind. Looking at the water moving so free, makes it wonderful to be by the sea.

Father Said

A father to me is as strong as can be. Looking at this man, and I can see the joy in his face for having me. Sometimes it's hard you see, to work and raise a family. It's happiness in a family. I know this is true, don't let the bad things get next to you.

Some People

People always say what they would do, talking about things they know aren't true, for me it's always been that way, always trying to stay away. From pushing and shoving of times of the pass. Somehow always falling on my ass. Getting up from the fall I always do, continuing to stand, what else can we do.

If I,

Sunny days, Pillowing nights thinking of the day to make my flight. If I could start let's begin, let's go all the way to the end, starting with death you're born again, signals and signs begin,s the end. Looking around you feel cold, look in the mirror, starting old. As you go backward in time you start to feel, asking yourself is this really real. A voice from nowhere speaks to you and says, don't worry, it's almost the beginning for you.

Scent of a Flower

The smell of a flower so fresh, so new. When I smell the scent, I think of you. From the first day we met, I had this feeling deep inside of me, but now we're together I feel so free. I'm floating so high, so high, you see. It's because of you, begin here with me.

A Mother's Love

Mothers are the most important people in the world today. Taking the hand of a child to guide them the right way. This is important you see, molding a child to what you desire them to be. Don't get me wrong father,s are important too. But the love of a Mother can never be matched in keeping that child on the right track.

Capricorn

Capricorn
December 22 - January 19

Symbol: The Goat

Ruling Planet: Saturn

Ruling House: Tenth House of Career and Public Image

Key Traits: Traditional, down-to-earth, industrious, disciplined

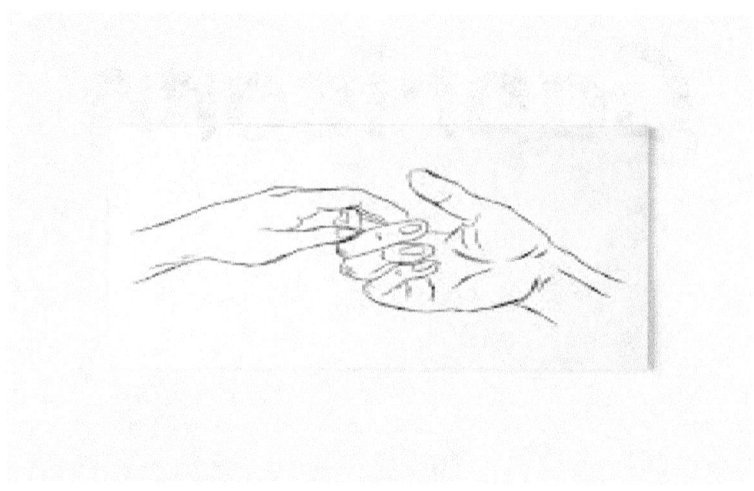

Confession of Love

For as many stars in the sky, my love for you will never die. For all the pain I feel in my life, somehow you always find a way to make it right. I feel so lucky, I really do, to have a lady as sweet as you.

A Kiss

The only wish for me is to have a kiss to set me free. Closing my eyes in my imagination I can see the flowers, the moon and one kiss from thy. My toes would tengo, my heart skips a beat, I open my eyes, I'm at your feet. Will you marry me I say real loud, to see you happy would make me so proud. To ask for your hand to enter my life. I would be very happy for you to be my wife.

Sitting Around

Sitting around like I do, can't help but wonder what to do. Should I do this or should I do that, the decision is hard and that's a fact. Feeling like the world is on my back, pushing real hard to get back on track. It's going to take awhile, but that's alright. I never was one to give up a fight. With all my courage in my hands I will win, because that's my plan.

Figure it Out

There is this feeling that won't go away, a certain kind of feeling I feel every day. Not bad or good, that's not what it's about. Thinking real hard, can't figure it out. Going through this I'd have to say, it's not a good way to start a day. Bad or good, have no doubt, take your time you'll figure it out.

Trying to Understand

Have you ever thought or wonder why we are born and then we die. But what happens between this time? Trying to be successful, meeting people saying Hi. Sometimes you think, who am I. As we go pass that person inside. Success is closer, open your eyes. And when we succeed, what do we do, we look for other successful things to do. Often good, Sometimes bad just be grateful for what we have.

Babies,

Babies being born today, look and act a different way. Smarter, stronger getting up on their knees, a lot earlier than we achieved. Walking so soon after being born to this life, thinking they're ready to challenge this life. Fear is something they don't understand, pulling and picking with their cute little hands. But one day we know this is true. They will grow to succeed just like you.

The Game

How can I explain this game that is so different, but somehow the same. Don't do this, Don't do that. Being able to choose can affect the life around you. So make your decisions and when you do. Keep love in the family and things will come to you. Now remember and don't forget living your life is the greatest gift.

The Flight

Our souls are like a dove in the wind, Higher, Higher into the sky and then. Losing all sights and sound of this earthly bound. Entering a bright light, floating like the wind, approaching a new faze and then begins. The feeling is so warm, the smell is so sweet, the memories of people appear that you meet. Family, Friends, enemies and sins in one big sweep and then they end. Now is the time for you to know. A decision is made which way do you go.

(Wishing upon a Star, to follow where you are.)

In me,

All of these poems are in my head, trying to come out even in bed. So look over them and you will see that these poems are a part of me. Writing them is easy, you see. I just sit back and they come to me. Like right now I don't understand why I can't control my hand. It brings out things I can not see, with imagination and words it sets me free.

Authors History

Born in Michigan raised in the suburbs of Detroit and Chicago. My childhood was to my memory very good. I believe I was a lucky kid. With fun parents and very knowledgeable about life and the different personalities of the people we meet. Providing me with the tools that I needed to cope with this life. Faith and Belief, the strongest of the two. With many more as I grew. It's what moves me today. Lighting the torch for me to stay in life's race. I'm blessed for the love and understanding they shared with me. Writing has been a passion of mine for as long as I remember. I have never had any training or study involving writing. I just write what comes to me. Hope you enjoy the feeling.

" In life you will be faced with a series of God ordained opportunities, brilliantly disguised as problems and Challenges. "

Charle Udall,